**For my best girl, Timberly,
my son, Anthony,
my sweet Mom (editor-in-chief),
the many family and friends I'm
blessed to have, and for
YOU!**

Special thanks to Robin Hartman for all of your creative feedback.

Special mention to Marcel John for your scriptural expertise.

All rights reserved. No part of this publication may be reproduced or transmitted in any form or by any means, electronic, mechanical, photocopying, recording, or otherwise without written permission from the author. For permission requests, email the author at UNeedHim2@gmail.com.

Copyright © 2023 Melissa White. Printed in the United States of America. First Edition, 2023.

ISBN: 978-1-946467-13-3 (Paperback)

ISBN: 978-1-946467-17-1 (Hardcover)

ISBN: 978-1-946467-14-0 (eBook)

Library of Congress Control Number: 2023905470

Scripture quotations taken from the (NASB®) New American Standard Bible®, Copyright © 1960, 1971, 1977, 1995 by The Lockman Foundation. Used by permission. All rights reserved. www.lockman.org and (MSG) THE MESSAGE: The Bible in Contemporary Language Copyright © 1993, 2002, 2018 by Eugene H. Peterson. All rights reserved. Used by permission of NavPress. Represented by Tyndale House Publishers.

Friends and family drawings and photos are used by permission. Any other resemblance to real persons, living or dead, except for the biblical characters represented is purely coincidental and unintentional.

The Night Before Easter in Jerusalem

Written and Illustrated by
Melissa White

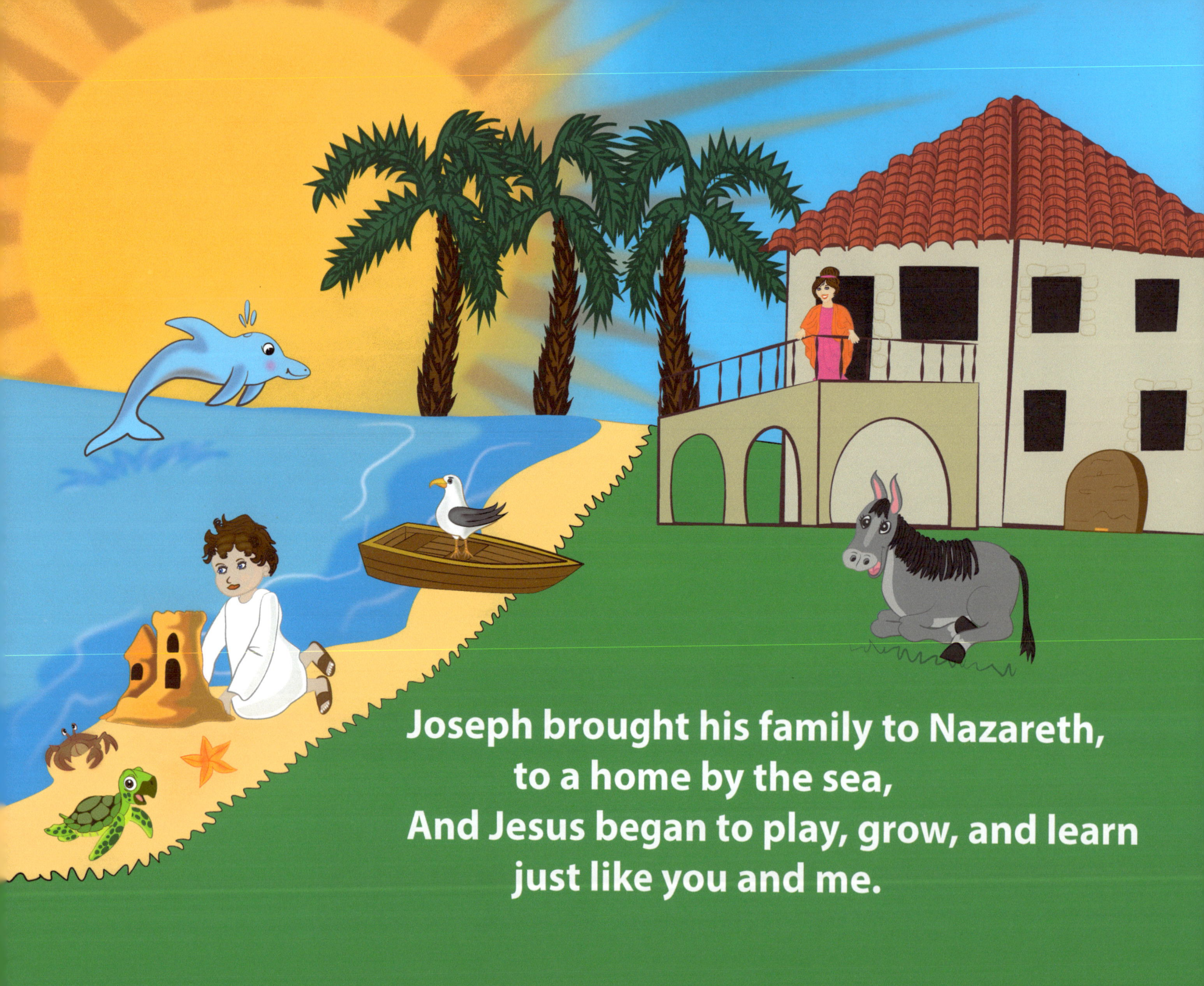

Joseph brought his family to Nazareth,
to a home by the sea,
And Jesus began to play, grow, and learn
just like you and me.

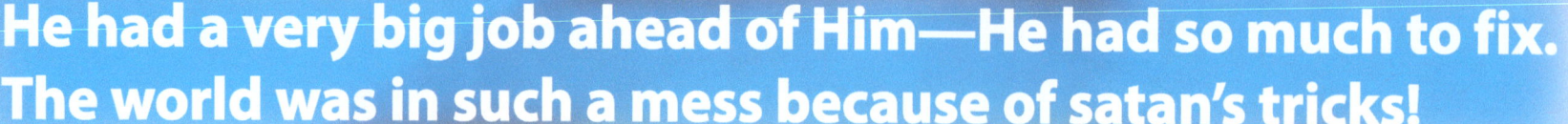

He had a very big job ahead of Him—He had so much to fix. The world was in such a mess because of satan's tricks!

You see, God created satan as a beautiful angel, and heaven was his home,

But when he tried to steal the kingdom, he was cast out and fell to earth to roam.

He took some of God's other angels with him—
they'd been foolish to think he'd win.
And they were all stripped of their splendor
and glory as a result of their sin.

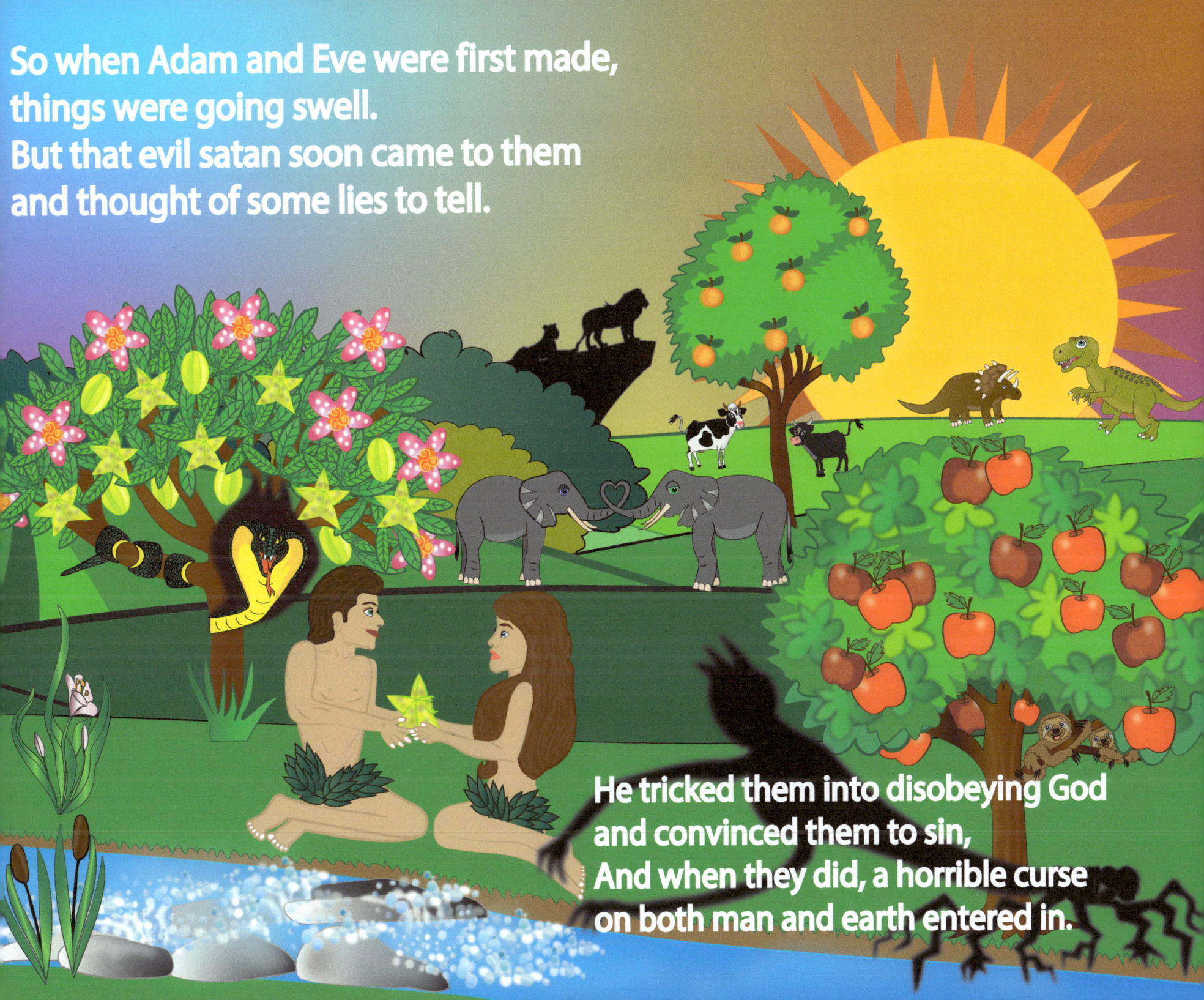

After He was born, He spent 33 years teaching us how to live life as we should. The Bible tells us that during this time, He went about healing and doing good.

This man was blind and had to beg for things, but He gave him sight like only He can bring.

Many had been listening to Him teach all day.
He wanted to feed them before sending them away.
So He multiplied a boy's small lunch,
and there wasn't an empty belly in the bunch.

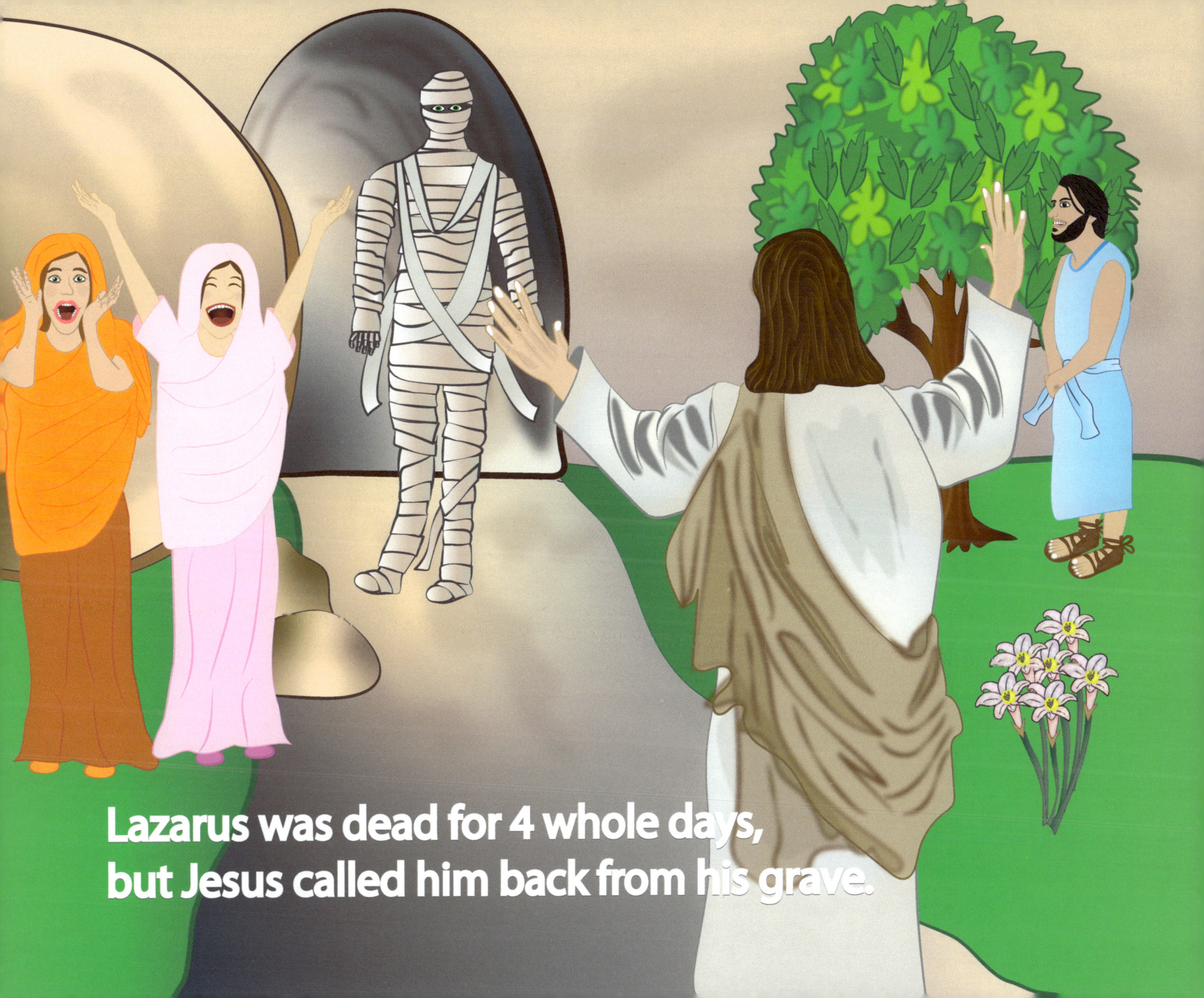

During a huge storm, He came walking to His friends right across the sea! Peter cried, "If that's really You, Lord, then please send for me!"

Even children came to meet Him.
One day the disciples tried to shoo them away,
But Jesus fussed at them and commanded
that they let the children stay.

He said His kingdom belongs
to children, and everyone
needs child-like faith to get in!

Then He gathered the kids
into His strong embrace,
And spent time
blessing each of them
face to face.

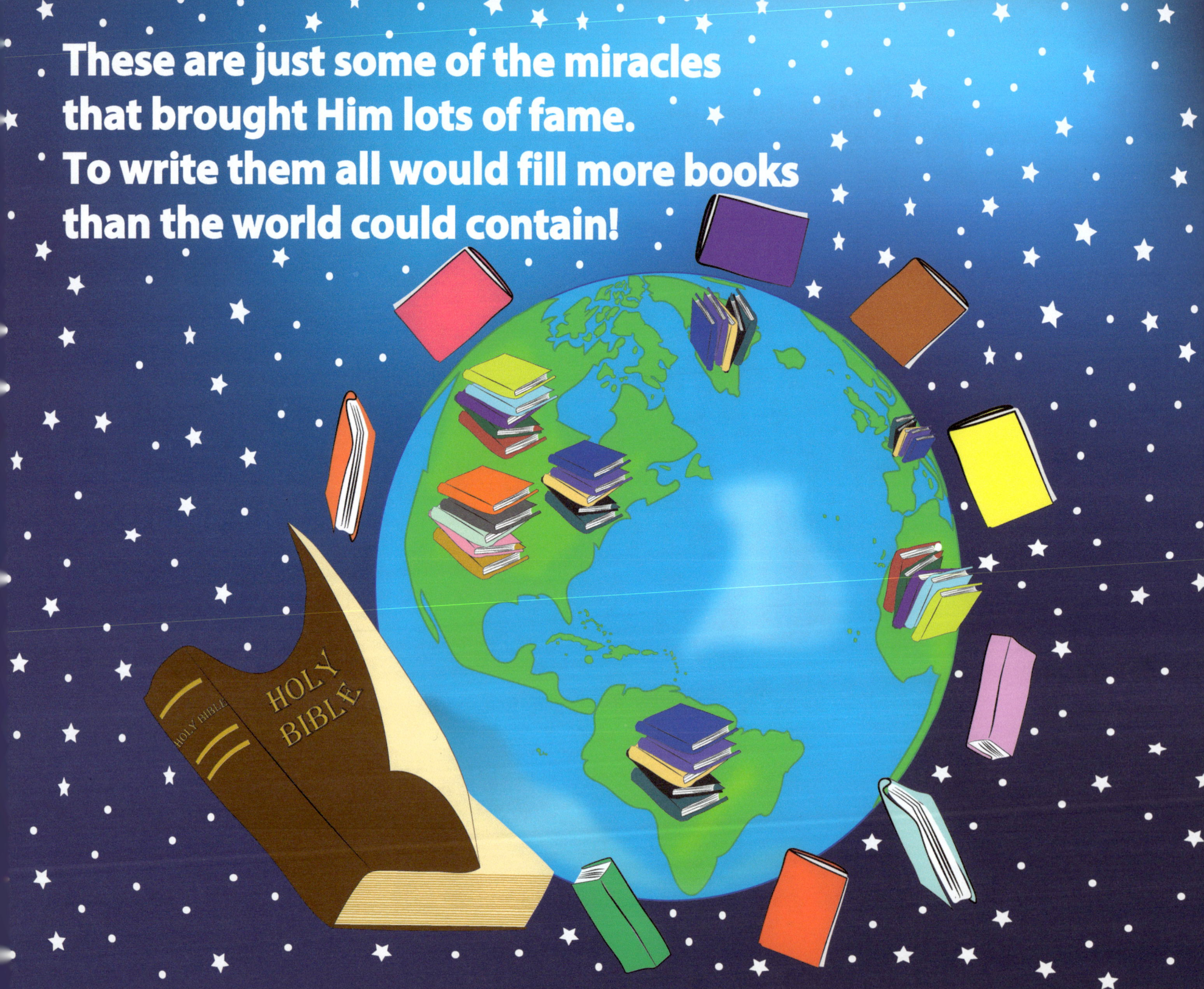

These are just some of the miracles that brought Him lots of fame.
To write them all would fill more books than the world could contain!

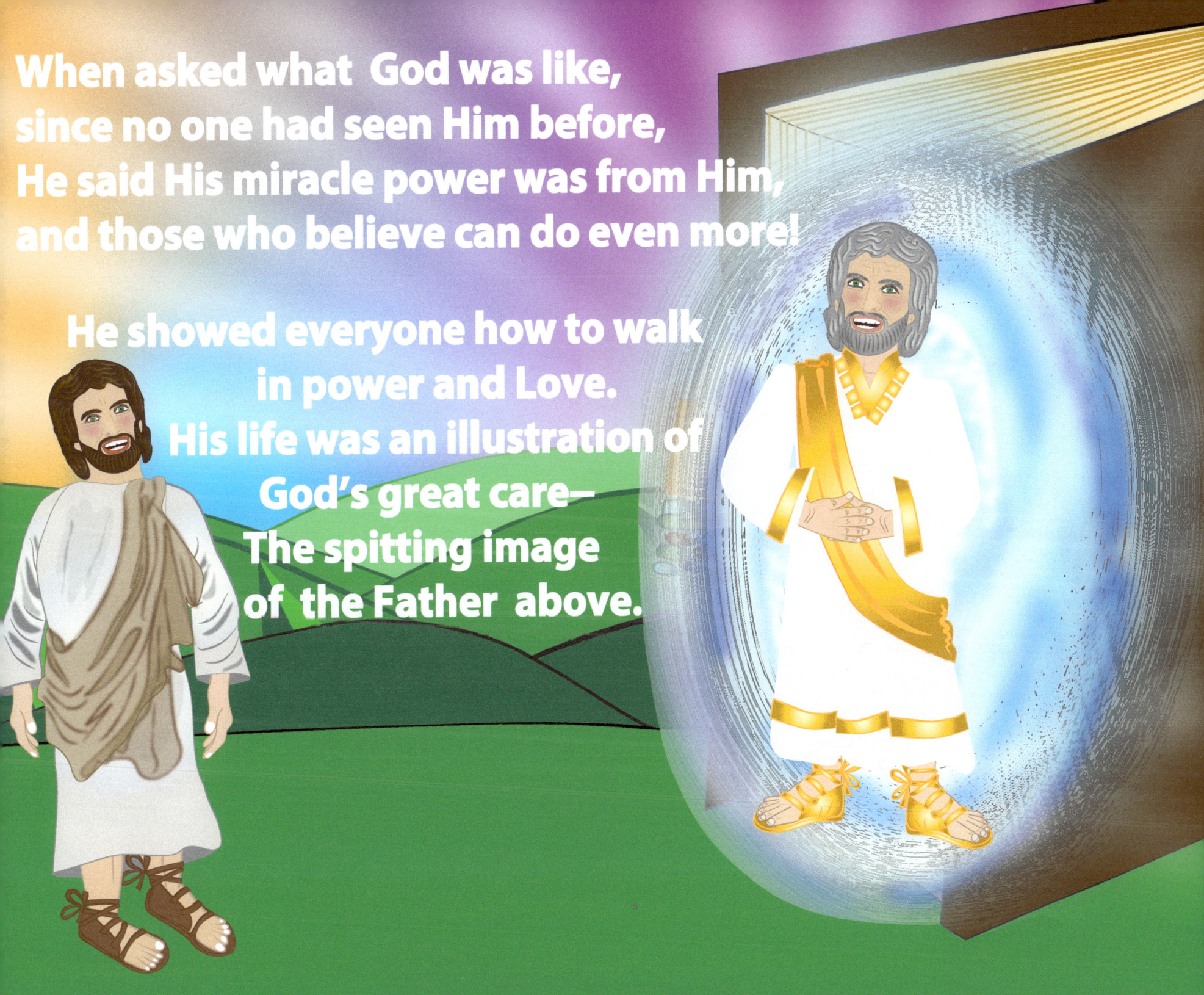

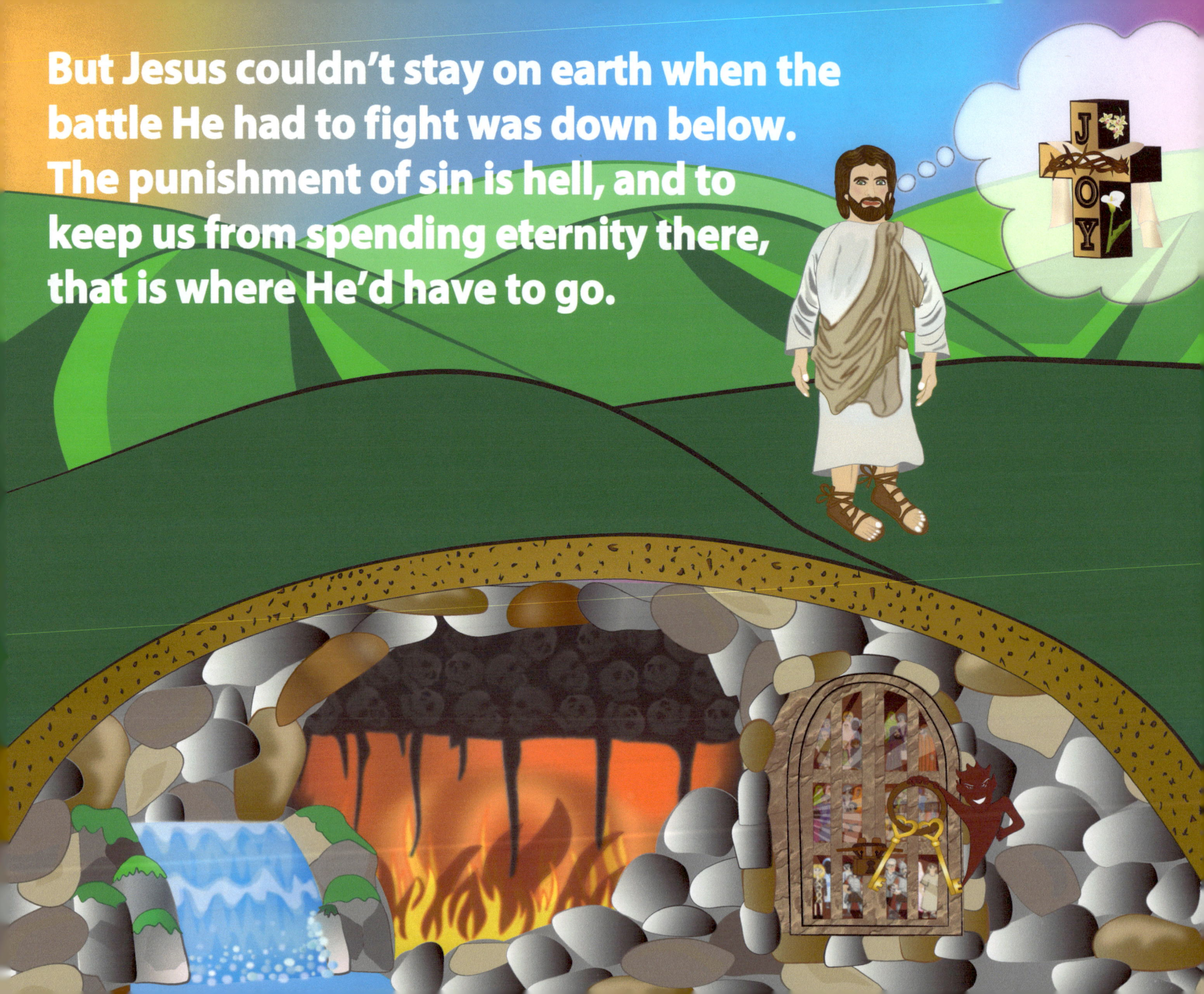
But Jesus couldn't stay on earth when the battle He had to fight was down below. The punishment of sin is hell, and to keep us from spending eternity there, that is where He'd have to go.

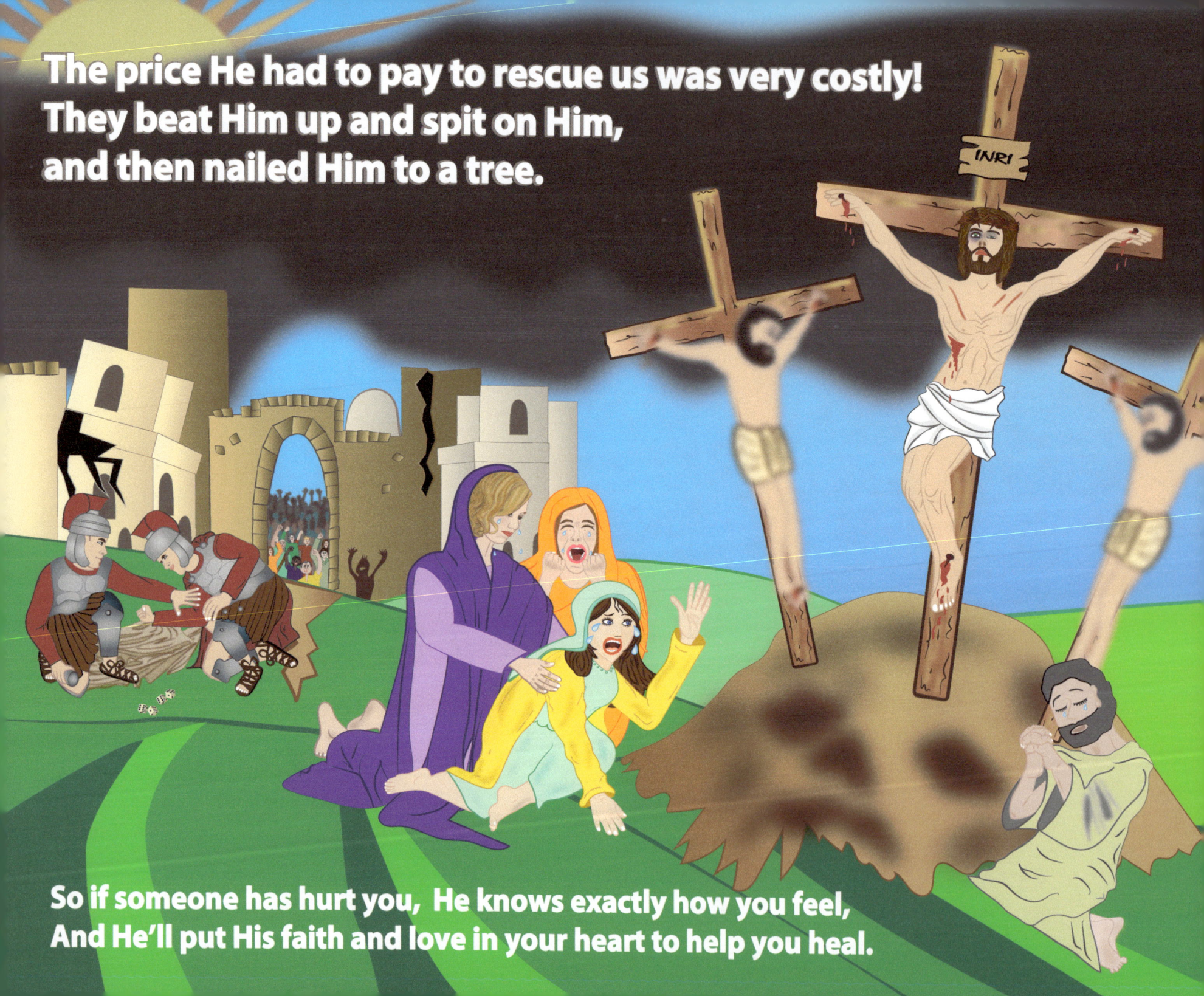

Happy Easter

May Easter be a time to remember that though
His suffering was very bad,
He braved it to make right all that
had gone wrong, and we shouldn't be sad.

Instead, let's do our best to live in all that He's restored,
and be thankful for the empty tomb as we
celebrate our risen Lord!

Dear Reader:

As you can see, Jesus lived quite the life! And He died quite the death. But then He arose from the dead as a Victor to share His victory with us. He is King of His kingdom on earth and in heaven. And it is a kingdom that we join by faith and prayer. It is a kingdom of peace, of protection, of love, of everything that we need. Life is full of happy and sad, good times and bad, joy and sorrow, and that is the same for everyone. Jesus righted all that went wrong, but we still have to trust Him to apply it to our lives. The Good News is that in His kingdom we have hope. We have Him on our side. It makes everything better than it would be without Him. We can't see Him but we can know He is always with us because He promises to be.

Remember, we can pray anytime, anywhere, about anything, and receive His help in our lives. We can pray out loud or with just a whisper, and He'll hear us. Sometimes He fixes things quickly and sometimes slowly. Sometimes we have a part to do in situations, and sometimes He does it all while we wait, but He is always faithful. (Even when we can't see Him working, like the quiet Saturday, He is battling satan on our behalf.)

To best gain access to His kingdom, we need to be born again, like you read in the story. *Our new birth is by the Holy Spirit with Love that is faithful and pure.* When we invite Jesus into our lives, we become part of the family of God with the Spirit's help. If you would like to pray for Jesus to live in your heart, here is a great prayer:

Father God, Holy Spirit, and Lord Jesus, thank You for loving me so much that Jesus died on the cross for my sins. Please forgive me for the wrong things I have done and wash my heart clean. I want to be best friends with You forever. Please show me how to hear and follow You every day. Thank You for never leaving me. I love You! In Jesus' Name, Amen!

When Jesus was lifted up, He promised that He would prepare a place for us, and He will return to get us. Jesus will come back for us at the exact time that Father God plans for Him to come. That is exciting news! I pray that you will continue to learn about Him and develop your friendship with Him. I will keep writing if you keep reading!

**Your friend,
Melissa**

Jesus' Childhood:

But when Herod died, behold, an angel of the Lord appeared in a dream to Joseph in Egypt, and said, "Get up, take the Child and His mother, and go into the land of Israel; for those who sought the Child's life are dead." So, Joseph got up, took the Child and His mother, and came into the land of Israel. Then after being warned by God in a dream, he left for the regions of Galilee, and came and lived in a city called Nazareth. This was to fulfill what was spoken through the prophets: "He shall be called a Nazarene." *Matthew 2:19-23 NAS*

Then, after three days they (Joseph and Mary) found Him in the temple, sitting in the midst of the teachers, both listening to them and asking them questions. And He went down with them and came to Nazareth, and He continued in subjection to them; and His mother treasured all these things in her heart. And Jesus kept increasing in wisdom and stature, and in favor with God and men. *Luke 2:46, 51-52 NAS*

Satan Cast Out of Heaven:

Your pomp and the music of your harps have been brought down to Sheol; How you have fallen from heaven, O star of the morning, son of the dawn! You have been cut down to the earth, you who have weakened the nations! But you said in your heart, 'I will ascend to heaven; I will raise my throne above the stars of God, I will make myself like the Most High.' Nevertheless, you will be thrust down to Sheol, to the recesses of the pit. *Isaiah 14:11-15 NAS*

And there was war in heaven, Michael and his angels waging war with the dragon. The dragon and his angels waged war, and they were not strong enough, and there was no longer a place found for them in heaven. And the great dragon was thrown down, the serpent of old who is called the devil and satan, who deceives the whole world; he was thrown down to the earth, and his angels were thrown down with him. So the dragon was enraged with the woman, and went off to make war with the rest of her children, who keep the commandments of God and hold to the testimony of Jesus. *Revelation 12:7-9,17 NAS*

And He said to them, "I was watching Satan fall from heaven like lightning." *Luke 10:18 NAS*

Now judgment is upon this world; now the ruler of this world will be cast out. *John 12:31 NAS*

Creation of Man and His Fall in the Garden:

Then God said, "Let Us make man in Our image, according to Our likeness; and let them rule over the fish of the sea and over the birds of the sky and over the cattle and over all the earth, and over every creeping thing that creeps on the earth." God created man in His own image, in the image of God He created him; male and female He created them. *Genesis 1:26-27 NAS*

Then the LORD God formed man of dust from the ground and breathed into his nostrils the breath of life; and man became a living being. The LORD God commanded the man, saying, "From any tree of the garden you may eat freely; but from the tree of the knowledge of good and evil you shall not eat, for in the day that you eat from it you will surely die." Then the LORD God said, "It is not good for the man to be alone; I will make him a helper suitable for him." So the LORD God caused a deep sleep to fall upon the man, and he slept; then He took one of his ribs and closed up the flesh at that place. The LORD God fashioned into a woman the rib which He had taken from the man and brought her to the man. *Genesis 2:7, 16-18, 21-22 NAS*

Now the serpent was more crafty than any beast of the field which the LORD God had made. And he said to the woman, "Indeed, has God said, 'You shall not eat from any tree of the garden'?" The woman said to the serpent, "From the fruit of the trees of the garden we may eat; but from the fruit of the tree which is in the middle of the garden, God has said, 'You shall not eat from it or touch it, or you will die.'" The serpent said to the woman, "You surely will not die! For God knows that in the day you eat from it your eyes will be opened, and you will be like God, knowing good and evil." When the woman saw that the tree was good for food, and that it was a delight to the eyes, and that the tree was desirable to make one wise, she took from its fruit and ate; and she gave also to her husband with her, and he ate. Then the eyes of both of them were opened, and they knew that they were naked; and they sewed fig leaves together and made themselves loin coverings. Then to Adam He said, "Because you have listened to the voice of your wife, and have eaten from the tree about which I commanded you, saying, 'You shall not eat from it'; Cursed is the ground because of you." *Genesis 3:1-7, 17 NAS*

Satan's Stolen Authority, God's Plan of Redemption, Jesus to Our Rescue:

We know that we are of God, and that the whole world lies in the power of the evil one. *1 John 5:19 NAS*

...in which you formerly walked according to the course of this world, according to the prince of the power of the air, of the spirit that is now working in the sons of disobedience. *Ephesians 2:2 NAS*

...in whose case the god of this world has blinded the minds of the unbelieving so that they might not see the light of the gospel of the glory of Christ, who is the image of God. *2 Corinthians 4:4 NAS*

For I have come down from heaven, not to do My own will, but the will of Him who sent Me. *John 6:38 NAS*

I am the door; if anyone enters through Me, he will be saved, and will go in and out and find pasture. The thief comes only to steal and kill and destroy; I came that they may have life, and have it abundantly. *John 10:9-10 NAS*

It cost God plenty to get you...He paid with Christ's sacred blood. He died like an unblemished, sacrificial lamb. And this was no afterthought. Even though it has only lately become public knowledge, God always knew He was going to do this for you. It's because of this sacrificed Messiah, whom God then raised from the dead and glorified, that you trust God, that you know you have a future in God. *1 Peter 1:18-21 MSG*

But when the fullness of the time came, God sent forth His Son, born of a woman, born under the Law, so that He might redeem those who were under the Law, that we might receive the adoption as sons. Because you are sons, God has sent forth the Spirit of His Son into our hearts, crying, "Abba! Father!" *Galatians 4:4-6 NAS*

But we do see Him who was made for a little while lower than the angels, namely, Jesus, because of the suffering of death crowned with glory and honor, so that by the grace of God He might taste death for everyone. Therefore, since the children share in flesh and blood, He Himself likewise also partook of the same, that through death He might render powerless him who had the power of death, that is, the devil. *Hebrews 2:9,14 NAS*

For even the Son of Man did not come to be served, but to serve, and to give His life a ransom for many. *Mark 10:45 NAS*

...fixing our eyes on Jesus, the author and perfecter of faith, who for the joy set before Him endured the cross, despising the shame, and has sat down at the right hand of the throne of God. For consider Him who has endured such hostility by sinners against Himself, so that you will not grow weary and lose heart. *Hebrews 12:2-3 NAS*

And Jesus came up and spoke to them, saying, "All authority has been given to Me in heaven and on earth." *Matthew 28:18 NAS*

Behold, I have given you authority to tread on serpents and scorpions, and over all the power of the enemy, and nothing will injure you. *Luke 10:19 NAS*

Salvation in Christ/Born Again:

Jesus said to him, "I am the Way, and the Truth, and the Life; no one comes to the Father but through Me. *John 14:6 NAS*

For the wages of sin is death, but the free gift of God is eternal life in Christ Jesus our Lord. *Romans 6:23 NAS*

Jesus answered and said to him, "Truly, truly, I say to you, unless one is born again he cannot see the kingdom of God. Unless a person submits to a baptism into a new life—it's not possible to enter God's kingdom. When you look at a baby, it's just that: a body you can look at and touch. But the person who takes shape within is formed by something you can't see and touch—the Spirit—and becomes a living spirit. So don't be so surprised when I tell you that you have to be 'born from above'—out of this world, so to speak. You know well enough how the wind blows this way and that. You hear it rustling through the trees, but you have no idea where it comes from or where it's headed next. That's the way it is with everyone 'born from above' by the wind of God, the Spirit of God." *John 3:3, 5-8 NAS, MSG*

The Ministry and Miracles of Jesus:

When He began His ministry, Jesus Himself was about thirty years of age. *Luke 3:23 NAS*

You know of Jesus of Nazareth, how God anointed Him with the Holy Spirit and with power, and how He went about doing good and healing all who were oppressed by the devil, for God was with Him. *Acts 10:38 NAS*

As He passed by, He saw a man blind from birth. He spat on the ground, and made clay of the spittle, and applied the clay to his eyes, and said to him, "Go, wash in the pool of Siloam" (which is translated, Sent). So he went away and washed, and came back seeing. *John 9:1, 6-7 NAS*

And there came a man named Jairus, and he was an official of the synagogue; and he fell at Jesus' feet and began to implore Him to come to his house; for he had an only daughter, about twelve years old, and she was dying. While He was still speaking, someone came from the house of the synagogue official, saying, "Your daughter has died; do not trouble the Teacher anymore." But when Jesus heard this, He answered him, "Do not be afraid any longer; only believe, and she will be made well." He took her by the hand and called, saying, "Child, arise!" And her spirit returned, and she got up immediately; and He gave orders for something to be given her to eat. *Luke 8:41-42, 49-50, 54-55 NAS*

So Jesus, again being deeply moved within, came to the tomb. Now it was a cave, and a stone was lying against it. Jesus said, "Remove the stone." Martha, the sister of the deceased, said to Him, "Lord, by this time there will be a stench, for he has been dead four days." Jesus said to her, "Did I not say to you that if you believe, you will see the glory of God?" So they removed the stone. Then Jesus raised His eyes, and said, "Father, I thank You that You have heard Me. I knew that You always hear Me; but because of the people standing around I said it, so that they may believe that You sent Me." When He had said these things, He cried out with a loud voice, "Lazarus, come forth." The man who had died came forth, bound hand and foot with wrappings, and his face was wrapped around with a cloth. Jesus said to them, "Unbind him, and let him go." Therefore, many of the Jews who came to Mary, and saw what He had done, believed in Him. *John 11:38-45 NAS*

"There is a lad here who has five barley loaves and two fish, but what are these for so many people?" Jesus said, "Have the people sit down." Now there was much grass in the place. So the men sat down, in number about five thousand. Jesus then took the loaves, and having given thanks, He distributed to those who were seated; likewise, also of the fish as much as they wanted. When they were filled, He said to His disciples, "Gather up the leftover fragments so that nothing will be lost." So they gathered them up, and filled twelve baskets with fragments from the five barley loaves which were left over by those who had eaten. *John 6:9-13 NAS*

Immediately He made the disciples get into the boat and go ahead of Him to the other side, while He sent the crowds away. After He had sent the crowds away, He went up on the mountain by Himself to pray; and when it was evening, He was there alone. But the boat was already a long distance from the land, battered by the waves; for the wind was contrary. And in the fourth watch of the night He came to them, walking on the sea. When the disciples saw Him walking on the sea, they were terrified, and said, "It is a ghost!" And they cried out in fear. But immediately Jesus spoke to them, saying, "Take courage, it is I; do not be afraid." Peter said to Him, "Lord, if it is You, command me to come to You on the water." And He said, "Come!" And Peter got out of the boat, and walked on the water and came toward Jesus. But seeing the wind, he became frightened, and beginning to sink, he cried out, "Lord, save me!" Immediately Jesus stretched out His hand and took hold of him, and said to him, "You of little faith, why did you doubt?" When they got into the boat, the wind stopped. And those who were in the boat worshiped Him, saying, "You are certainly God's Son!" *Matthew 14:22-33 NAS*

And He got up and rebuked the wind and said to the sea, "Hush, be still." And the wind died down and it became perfectly calm. *Mark 4:39 NAS*

One day children were brought to Jesus in the hope that He would lay hands on them and pray over them. The disciples shooed them off. But Jesus intervened: "Let the children alone, don't prevent them from coming to me. God's kingdom is made up of people like these." After laying hands on them, He left. *Matthew 19:13-15 MSG*

And He called a child to Himself and set him before them, and said, "Truly I say to you, unless you are converted and become like children, you will not enter the kingdom of heaven. Whoever then humbles himself as this child, he is the greatest in the kingdom of heaven. And whoever receives one such child in My name receives Me." *Matthew 18:2-5 NAS*

And there are also many other things which Jesus did, which if they were written in detail, I suppose that even the world itself would not contain the books that would be written. *John 21:25 NAS*

Philip said to Him, "Lord, show us the Father, and it is enough for us." Jesus said to him, "Have I been so long with you, and yet you have not come to know Me, Philip? He who has seen Me has seen the Father; how can you say, 'Show us the Father'? The Father abiding in Me does His works. He who believes in Me, the works that I do, he will do also; and greater works than these he will do; because I go to the Father." *John 14:8-10, 12 NAS*

And He is the radiance of His glory and the exact representation of His nature, and upholds all things by the word of His power. *Hebrews 1:3 NAS*

Jesus' Crucifixion and Battle:

Then they spat in His face and beat Him with their fists; and others slapped Him. *Matthew 26:67 NAS*

So Pilate took Jesus and had Him whipped. The soldiers, having braided a crown from thorns, set it on His head and approached Him with, "Hail, King of the Jews!" Then they greeted Him with slaps in the face. When the high priests and police saw Him, they shouted in a frenzy, "Crucify! Crucify! Kill him! Kill him! Crucify him!" Pilate caved in to their demand. He turned Him over to be crucified. They took Jesus away. Jesus went out to the place called Skull Hill (the name in Hebrew is Golgotha), where they crucified Him, and with Him two others, one on each side, Jesus in the middle. Pilate wrote a sign and had it placed on the cross. It read: JESUS THE NAZARENE THE KING OF THE JEWS. The Roman soldiers took His clothes and divided them up, but His robe was seamless, a single piece of weaving, so they said to each other, "Let's not tear it up. Let's throw dice to see who gets it." While the soldiers were looking after themselves, Jesus' mother, his aunt, Mary the wife of Clopas, and Mary Magdalene stood at the foot of the cross. Jesus saw His mother and the disciple He loved standing near her. He said to his mother, "Woman, here is your son." Then to the disciple, "Here is your mother." From that moment the disciple accepted her as his own mother. One of the soldiers stabbed Him in the side with his spear. Joseph and Nicodemus took Jesus' body and, following the Jewish burial custom, wrapped it in linen with the spices. There was a garden near the place He was crucified, and in the garden a new tomb in which no one had yet been placed. So, they placed Jesus in it. *John 19 MSG*

It was now about the sixth hour, and darkness fell over the whole land until the ninth hour, because the sun was obscured; and the veil of the temple was torn in two. *Luke 23:44-45 NAS* ...and the earth shook and the rocks were split. *Matthew 27:51 NAS*

And He said to him, "Truly I say to you, today you shall be with Me in Paradise." *Luke 23:43 NAS*

Now the poor man died and was carried away by the angels to Abraham's bosom; and the rich man also died and was buried. In Hades he lifted up his eyes, being in torment, and saw Abraham far away and Lazarus in his bosom. And besides all this, between us and you there is a great chasm fixed, so that those who wish to come over from here to you will not be able, and that none may cross over from there to us.' *Luke 16:22-23, 26 NAS*

He went and proclaimed God's salvation to earlier generations who ended up in the prison of judgment because they wouldn't listen. You know, even though God waited patiently all the days that Noah built his ship, only a few were saved then, eight to be exact—saved from the water by the water. *1 Peter 3:9-20 NAS*

Therefore it says, "WHEN HE ASCENDED ON HIGH, HE LED CAPTIVE A HOST OF CAPTIVES AND HE GAVE GIFTS TO MEN." *Ephesians 4:8 NAS*

When He had disarmed the rulers and authorities, He made a public display of them, having triumphed over them through Him. *Colossians 2:15 NAS*

Victory Over Death/Ascension:

"Do not be afraid; I am the first and the last, and the living One; and I was dead, and behold, I am alive forevermore, and I have the keys of death and of Hades." *Revelation 1:17-18 NAS*

Early in the morning on the first day of the week, while it was still dark, the stone was moved away from the entrance. Peter and the other disciple left immediately for the tomb. They ran, neck and neck. Simon Peter observed the linen cloths lying there, and the kerchief used to cover His head not lying with the linen cloths but separate, neatly folded by itself. *John 20:1-13 NAS*

Now after the Sabbath, as it began to dawn toward the first day of the week, Mary Magdalene and the other Mary came to look at the grave. And behold, a severe earthquake had occurred, for an angel of the Lord descended from heaven and came and rolled away the stone and sat upon it. And his appearance was like lightning, and his clothing as white as snow. The guards shook for fear of him and became like dead men. The angel said to the women, "Do not be afraid; for I know that you are looking for Jesus who has been crucified. He is not here, for He has risen, just as He said. Come, see the place where He was lying." *Matthew 28:2-6 NAS*

So when it was evening on that day, the first day of the week, and when the doors were shut where the disciples were, for fear of the Jews, Jesus came and stood in their midst and said to them, "Peace be with you." And when He had said this, He showed them both His hands and His side. The disciples then rejoiced when they saw the Lord. So Jesus said to them again, "Peace be with you; as the Father has sent Me, I also send you." *John 20:19-21 NAS*

The first account I composed, Theophilus, about all that Jesus began to do and teach, until the day when He was taken up to heaven after He had by the Holy Spirit given orders to the apostles whom He had chosen. To these He also presented Himself alive after His suffering, by many convincing proofs, appearing to them over a period of forty days and speaking of the things concerning the kingdom of God. And after He had said these things, He was lifted up while they were looking on, and a cloud received Him out of their sight. And as they were gazing intently into the sky while He was going, behold, two men in white clothing stood beside them. They also said, "Men of Galilee, why do you stand looking into the sky? This Jesus, who has been taken up from you into heaven, will come in just the same way as you have watched Him go into heaven." *Acts 1:1-3, 9-11 NAS*

Trust me. There is plenty of room for you in my Father's home. If that weren't so, would I have told you that I'm on my way to get a room ready for you? And if I'm on my way to get your room ready, I'll come back and get you so you can live where I live. *John 14:1-3 MSG*

PS:

I chose to include a broader account of events in my story, going all the way back to satan's exile from heaven and man's fall after creation to explain why Jesus had to come rescue us, but there are other events in His life and the Easter story that you can read about. Some of them include:

- *His transfiguration on the Mount of Olives (Matthew 17:2)*
- *Jesus' triumphant arrival in Jerusalem on Palm Sunday (Mark 11:1-11)*
- *the Last Supper (Matthew 26:17-29)*
- *Jesus washing the disciples' feet (John 13:2-17)*
- *Judas betraying Jesus (Matthew 26:14-16)*
- *the Garden of Gethsemane (Matthew 26:36-46)*
- *Peter cutting the ear off a soldier and Jesus putting it back on (John 18:10)*
- *Peter denying Jesus and Jesus comforting Peter afterwards (Luke 22:54-62, John 21:15-25)*
- *Jesus appearing to the disciples lots of times after His resurrection (Mark 16:9, Matthew 28:9-10, Luke 24:13-32, John 21:1-14, 1 Corinthians 15:6, etc.)*

and many others.

    -MW